KU-519-380

WHAT'S THAT BIRD?

A Guide to British Birds

by Peter Hayman and Michael Everett

Contents

Cover illustration: male stonechats

© RSPB 1977 & 1978

Published by the Royal Society for the Protection of Birds
The Lodge, Sandy, Bedfordshire SG19 2DL

How to see Birds

When we collaborated in the series "What's that bird?", for *Birds* magazine, Peter Hayman and I set out to produce a step-by-step identification guide to commoner British birds, season by season and habitat by habitat. Using the technique so successfully pioneered by Peter in *The Birdlife of Britain* we tried to show not only diagnostic plumage features, but also how birds can be recognised by their shapes, the ways in which they move and the things they do. With a large format to work to we were also able to show whole groups of similar birds side-by-side. Now that the series has been brought together in book form we have the chance to add some comments on the art of bird identification.

Soon after the last part of the series had been completed, I went to the United States for the first time and very soon found myself amid a whole galaxy of completely new birds — over 70 in the first twenty-four hours, in fact. Suddenly, I was back in the shoes of the beginner and realised that there was no quick and easy way to get to know all these new birds: it would take time and patience and I knew I had no hope of identifying everything at first sight, nor of instantly learning and remembering all the new plumage features, shapes, movements and calls which confronted me. I was quite sharply reminded of those very things Peter and I had in mind when working on our series — patience, the need for careful observation and, above all, the need to learn slowly and thoroughly. I have always thought it wrong to try and produce "instant birdwatchers" — perhaps there has been too much of a trend recently towards making people think they can become expert at bird identification in just a year or so. I believe there is a lot of truth in the old adage about learning to walk before you run!

So where should you begin, and how? You can of course find and watch birds anywhere, but the best place to begin is at home — in your garden or local park, or within a mile or two of where you live. Get to know your local birds first — and learn them thoroughly. Start by getting to know their distinguishing marks — their basic colour patterns and most obvious features; watch out for wingbars, white outer tail-feathers, white rumps and so on; and remember that in a lot of birds the males and females are not alike — and that their young may be different again. Note too when you see them — some birds will be with you all the year round, while others appear only in summer or winter and still others may only pass through your area in spring or autumn.

Pay attention too to the shape of each bird — how it looks when on the ground, when perched and when flying, and note too how it moves on the ground and in the air. There are some birds which you will find are unmistakable even if seen only in silhouette, and others which have such a distinctive way of running or flying that you will be able to name them easily once you know them. It is just as important to note *where* these birds are — which are found only in woodlands, or near water, and so on. Above all — don't "forget" your local birds and think that once you've probably seen them all you should ignore them: keep looking at them and, even after years have gone by, you'll be surprised at how many new things you will notice and learn. And if you know them really well, picking out that odd one or the occasional real rarity will be that much easier!

A sound knowledge of your local birds will stand you in good stead for stage two, which is when you start to look for birds further afield — on your holidays, perhaps, or in the course of other travels around. After all, many of "your" birds will be found in other areas too, and again knowing them will help you to find the new ones, or those in habitats you have not so far examined. As you see each new species, apply the same principles you used at home — learn them carefully so that you will know them again. Bit by bit, you will build up your basic knowledge and experience and your enjoyment of your hobby will grow accordingly. Don't worry about going to famous bird reserves like Minsmere in the very early stages — it is probably a mistake to plunge into that sort of birdwatching straight away. Better do the groundwork first and *then* start thinking about trips to the bird meccas and places where you might see lots of really unusual species. It will be much more enjoyable if you take it slowly — and you'll be a better observer too.

A note book is as important as a decent pair of binoculars. You will soon find that your memory is not as reliable as you thought and writing it down is much better than trying to keep it all in your head! Record what you see, and where, but also make notes on all the new things you find out about this or that species as you go along — habits, movements and of course plumage details. Although many books are called "field" or "pocket" guides, it is better not to refer to them when actually looking at birds: make notes and look up the book afterwards and in this way you will not only teach yourself to notice and record those all-important small details but you will avoid the all-too-common pitfall of trying to make your bird fit a picture in your book and consequently completely misidentifying it. You will notice that this book is too big to go in your pocket — we had that in mind when writing this series! You will of course want to build up a small collection of books to refer to — we have listed those we think will help you most opposite.

You will quickly find that there are thousands of other people who like watching and identifying birds — get to know some of them by joining your local bird club or natural history society, or your local RSPB members' group. If there are extra-mural classes on ornithology in your area, go along to these — you will learn a lot. It is important to meet and talk to people who share your interest, partly because you will have the opportunity to go out on field-meetings with others who will be happy to share their knowledge and experience with you. Soon you will meet "experts" or more advanced birdwatchers — learn all you can from them at every opportunity, because there is no better way to learn birds than from someone who really knows his subject. Don't be embarrassed if they seem to know vastly more than you do (after all, they were beginners once too . . .) and never be afraid to ask if you don't know: you will be pleasantly surprised at how helpful most birdwatchers will be if consulted over an identification problem and, like anyone else, they will like to show off their own expertise!

Books and Records

In writing this brief introductory section, I have deliberately stressed the basic first principles of birdwatching, most of them based on observations. But there is one more element which Peter and I have often discussed and which we can do little more than allude to in a book like this: that is sound. It will quickly become very obvious to you that birds make lots of noises — songs, calls and so on — which they use at different times for different reasons. Most of these calls are as unique to the birds making them as their plumage and other identification features and no "good" birdwatcher will ignore the evidence of his ears. *Listen,* then, as well as look: learn the songs and calls of your local birds at the same time as you learn them by sight, and with the same care and thoroughness — and you will soon find that voice is a vital key to bird identification. It is amazing how often a bird is found by ear, rather than by eye. Your bird books will help with their descriptions of songs and phonetic renderings of calls, but inevitably these only take you part of the way and some bird-song records will be very valuable too: some of the best are listed opposite. As with watching, so with listening — go out with someone who knows his bird-calls and you will learn more than any book or record will ever teach you.

I hope that these notes, plus those which follow alongside Peter Hayman's paintings, will help you to make a good start towards identifying birds — and towards learning more about them. I might perhaps add one last word . . . don't worry if you cannot put a name to a bird: the honest birdwatcher, however expert, will admit that he will not be able to identify every bird he sees (or hears). He will make mistakes, too, just as you are bound to do. That is all part of the fun of birdwatching.

Michael Everett

Identification

Birdlife of Britain by Peter Hayman and Philip Burton. Published by Mitchell Beazley in association with the RSPB. Guide to commonest European species with first-class illustrations.

Birds of Britain and Europe by Hermann Heinzel, Richard Fitter and John Parslow. Published by Collins. Practical paperback guide, covering almost all the species to be found in Europe, the Middle East and North Africa. Excellent distribution maps.

Field Guide to the Birds of Britain and Europe by Roger Peterson, Guy Mountfort and P A D Hollom. Published by Collins. Although the oldest field-guide it is probably the best illustrated.

Hamlyn Guide to Birds of Britain and Europe by Bertel Bruun & Arthur Singer. Published by Hamlyn. Paperback with illustrations opposite the text.

Popular Handbook of British Birds by P A D Hollom. Published by Witherby. Excellent source of background information about birds.

RSPB Guide to British Birds by David Saunders, illustrated by N W Cusa and Peter Hayman. Published by Hamlyn in association with the RSPB. Best field-guide for the novice because it is restricted to British species and thus avoids confusion.

RSPB Guide to Birdwatching by Peter Conder, published by Hamlyn in association with the RSPB.

Watching Birds by James Fisher and Jim Flegg. Published by T & A D Poyser.

Binoculars, Telescopes and Cameras. BTO Guide No 14.

Records

The Peterson Field Guide to the Bird Songs of Britain and Europe. 14 records covering 530 species. Available singly or as a set.

Bird Sounds in Close Up by Victor Lewis. 12″ LP.

Woodland and Garden Birds by Eric Simms. Two 12″ LPs (also in cassette).

Wild Track. Cassettes by John Kirby. Nine cassettes available individually.

All these books and records are available from RSPB Sales, The Lodge, Sandy, Bedfordshire SG19 2DL. Other titles and a wide range of garden bird equipment and gifts are also available. Catalogues on request.

Farmland in autumn and winter

Birds often form flocks in autumn. In flight these may be identified by the way in which the flocks are formed and fly. Look carefully at the flight patterns, the way in which birds move on the ground and at wing- and tail patterns.

Woodpigeon in flight: note neck patch and white wing mark.

Below: **lapwings** in flight.

Rooks in flight: more swept wing and looser in manner than crow.

Wood pigeon   **Stock dove**

to show differences below.

Woodpigeon: large size, white neck patch.

Wood pigeon: large size, white neck and wing patches, pink breast.

Stock dove: note black wing edges, no white above and black wing marks.

Stock dove: "all" grey. Stocky but finer shape than wood pigeon and shorter tail.

Woodpigeon, stock and **collared dove** in flight to show typical flight positions. Note straight wing of stock dove with short, dumpy build. Long tail and swept wing of **collared dove.**

Pale wing panels (compare with **wood pigeon**)

Collared dove: long tail, and grey and buff pattern unique in winter pigeons.

Swept-wing flight with flicky action unique.

Collared dove: note black collar.

Above (small) **jackdaw**, and rounded tail of **rook** shown in flight.

Jackdaw, rook and **carrion crow.** Crow squarer and more deliberate than **rook** in flight. **Jackdaw** quite jerky flight.

Rook: high forehead, bare face, trousered legs.

Jackdaw: grey nape, small, perky action.

Carrion crow: all black, stout with clean legs.

At night **barn owl** can look almost white in car headlights.

Pheasant: female smaller than male, buff coloured, long tail.

Barn owls: legs sometimes dangle in flight. All white below but individuals vary above. Some whiter, others much greyer than this bird. Slow, wavery flight.

Rear view of male when flushed. Rapid wingbeats followed by long glides.

Note black eyes in all white face mask.

Pheasant: male ring-necked variety. Red wattles. Long tail and bright plumage.

Below **partridge** in flight.

Grey partridge: male in flight. Note horseshoe patch or "blob" duller in female.

Moorhens are often found about field edges in winter. Flicking tail and flank stripe distinctive.

Red-legged partridge: red legs, striped flanks and face marks usually catch eye.

Grey partridge: male above has orange face, female duller. Compare difference in flank stripes with red-leg.

Red-legged partridge (above) rear and facing views.

From a car, **partridges** appear as round blobs in a field.

Above **red-legged partridge:** pale buff edges to feathers distinguish from partridge but difficult to see without practice.

Little owl: tiny, round-headed, undulating flight. Often on post.

Golden plover: above, typical flock shapes and lines.

Lapwing: in flight and below. Black and white in flight: crest obvious on ground.

Bullet head, yellowish, spotted plumage.

Golden plover: often alights (left) and shows wings before folding.

5

Thrushes and starlings in winter

All birds 1–7 drawn to scale

Blackbird: all black male (1) above. Brown female (2) below.

Starling (7) (above): blackish. Only bird to feed with open-bill probing.

Starling (right): characteristic sharp pointed shapes; short, rounded tail.

Blackbird

Starling: pointed wings, short tail.

Blackbird: broad wings long tail.

Starling gliding.

Starlings (above) in typical, bustling feeding behaviour.

Redwing (3) (below): small, dark eye stripe, rather angry look and red flanks.

Song thrush: orange underwing noticeable in flight.

Fieldfare and **mistle thrush** (below) have somewhat similar flight.

More spotted breast than **redwing**.

Song thrush (4): yellower than redwing. No obvious head marks

Redwing: small "red" wing, whiter underparts than song thrush.

Fieldfare: white underwing, buff breast, pale white belly.

Mistle thrush: large, broad wing. White underwing "all spotted" body.

Mistle thrush (5): huge size, long tail and wings, boldly spotted breast. Looks greyer than song thrush.

Fieldfare (6): grey head and rump, reddish back and black tail unlike other thrushes. Call 'chack'.

Fieldfare (above) and **redwing** in flight show pattern and typical flight posture.

Fieldfares: typical ragged flock.

Birds often seen in this position in field.

Fieldfare: grey head, rump, black tail.

Song thrush: overall yellow-brown.

Redwing: eyestripe, pale edges to wing feathers.

Mistle thrush: large size, note thin head. Pale rump and wing marks, white tips to tail.

Starlings: mass in flight over fields (below) and when off to roost. Thrushes usually in small flocks.

Finches, buntings, larks and dunnock in winter

All perched birds drawn to same scale

Corn bunting in flight: heavy wings, shorter tail and heavier head than skylark.

Flocks of mixed finches and buntings rise and fall over winter fields.

Above, **corn bunting**: large bulky bird, heavy bill and pale yellow buff plumage.

Skylark: compare size with finches. Fairly fine bill, buff with streaked plumage. Often crouches when feeding.

Skylark: (above and left) small parties often fly low over fields. Note white outer tail feathers and white trailing edge to wing.

Skylark showing typical angled wings and triangular tail.

Dunnock (right): grey head, fine bill, brown streaked back, delicate feeding methods.

Tree sparrow (below): rufous crown, white black-spotted cheek and white collar. Sexes look alike.

Yellowhammer: instantly recognisable by bright rufous rump. White outer tail feathers.

House sparrow. Female above, male right. Country sparrows may be much brighter than city birds.

Greenfinch (left and above): stout, faint greenish colour. Yellow especially on sides of tail. Dull juvenile shown, adults brighter.

Chaffinch (female): wings as male but plumage buff and brown. Note slight "crest".

Chaffinch (male): blue-grey head, pinkish underparts and black and white wings.

Brambling: grey-black head, combination of orange and white in wing. Wing marks like chaffinch.

Brambling: only finch with chaffinch-like wing marks and white rump. Note no white to tip of tail.

Yellowhammer (juvenile): similar to female.

Above and right juvenile **linnet**, very small, slim, bouncing flight. Faint white edges to wing feathers.

Chaffinch (female): white wing and tail marks with greenish rump.

7

Woods, fields and gardens in summer

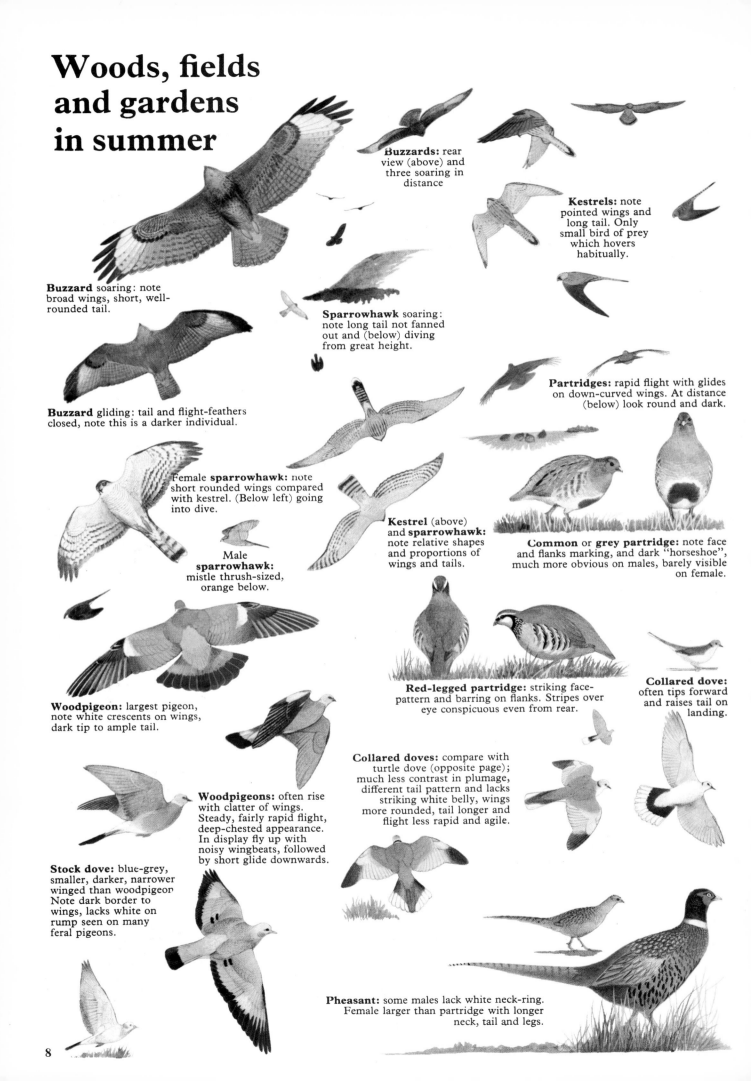

Buzzards: rear view (above) and three soaring in distance

Kestrels: note pointed wings and long tail. Only small bird of prey which hovers habitually.

Buzzard soaring: note broad wings, short, well-rounded tail.

Sparrowhawk soaring: note long tail not fanned out and (below) diving from great height.

Buzzard gliding: tail and flight-feathers closed, note this is a darker individual.

Partridges: rapid flight with glides on down-curved wings. At distance (below) look round and dark.

Female **sparrowhawk:** note short rounded wings compared with kestrel. (Below left) going into dive.

Male **sparrowhawk:** mistle thrush-sized, orange below.

Kestrel (above) and **sparrowhawk:** note relative shapes and proportions of wings and tails.

Common or **grey partridge:** note face and flanks marking, and dark "horseshoe", much more obvious on males, barely visible on female.

Woodpigeon: largest pigeon, note white crescents on wings, dark tip to ample tail.

Red-legged partridge: striking face-pattern and barring on flanks. Stripes over eye conspicuous even from rear.

Collared dove: often tips forward and raises tail on landing.

Woodpigeons: often rise with clatter of wings. Steady, fairly rapid flight, deep-chested appearance. In display fly up with noisy wingbeats, followed by short glide downwards.

Collared doves: compare with turtle dove (opposite page); much less contrast in plumage, different tail pattern and lacks striking white belly, wings more rounded, tail longer and flight less rapid and agile.

Stock dove: blue-grey, smaller, darker, narrower winged than woodpigeon Note dark border to wings, lacks white on rump seen on many feral pigeons.

Pheasant: some males lack white neck-ring. Female larger than partridge with longer neck, tail and legs.

Great (left) and **lesser spotted woodpecker** (centre) compared with **nuthatch** (right): all have rounded wings and markedly undulating flight.

Magpies: obvious long tail and white at wing-tips when flying.

Great spotted woodpecker: thrush-sized, strikingly pied; note "shoulder-patches".

Lesser spotted woodpecker: sparrow-sized barred above; often in very small trees among branches.

Magpie: only medium-sized, strikingly pied and long-tailed British bird.

Cuckoo: rather hawk-like. Does not hover, seldom glides. Wings flap below line of body, small head slightly above.

Jay below: note pinkish body, dark tail, wing-pattern, white rump and shape.

Jays: one bird flying out of wood is often followed by another; flight rather jerky.

Jackdaws: in flight all-dark; smaller than rooks or crows with faster wingbeats.

Male **green woodpecker** yellow below, green above red on head. Bill often pointing upwards.

Turtle doves: fast agile fliers, note white belly. From rear (above left) note chestnut wing-coverts and tail pattern.

Jackdaws: greyer than crows with dark crowns and "faces".

Green woodpecker: rear view, note yellow rump.

Female **green woodpecker:** habitually feeds on ground, very short legs, clumsy hops. Constantly turning head from side to side looking for danger.

Tawny owl: (left) characteristic upright stance and big, rounded head. Flight fairly slow and wholly silent. Note compactly built, big-headed, tail short and wings moderately long and rounded.

Male chaffinch: sings from tree perch, head back, repeated short song

Male greenfinch: sings in 'butterfly' display-flight overhead

Song thrush: sings from high perch, continuous loud song, repetitive phrases

Chaffinch: male (above), female (right), note wing and tail pattern

Male blackbird: sings from trees, rooftops, etc; rich, languid song

Male greenfinch: wheezes from tree, note (above) long wings and short tail in flight

Starling: jumbled song with head turning and wings flapping

Dunnocks: wing-flicking during display between pair

Robin: usually sings from high perch, often in tree

Starling: jaunty, waddling gait, probing with bill

Starlings: glide in to land

Blackbirds: swing down in jerky flight, cock tail on landing (female shown)

Song thrush: pauses between movements on ground

Starling: also has upright waddle, compare blackbird (right)

Blackbird: hops or runs, males often follow-chase in long runs across ground

Male robin: sings defiance at nearby rival

Robin: pauses to listen while feeding on ground

House sparrows: male (above) in low posture, female (below) in alert, upright hop

Dunnock: 'creeps' close to ground, flicking tail

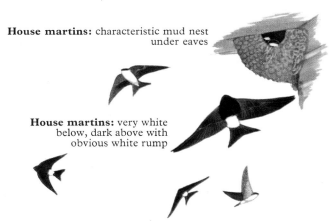

House martins: characteristic mud nest under eaves

House martins: very white below, dark above with obvious white rump

Swifts: aerial, fast-moving, all-dark and very long-winged; often in or over built-up areas

Swallows: habitually fly low and fast, feeding over fields and water

Swallow: from below, note throat pattern and tail streamers

Skylark: 'hangs' high overhead in continuous song and, (right) descends and finally dives to ground

Mistle thrush: in flight, large, heavy and long-tailed, note whitish underwing

Mistle thrush: larger than song thrush, less spotted below; sings from high tree

Skylark: rear view, note wing shape, white rear edge to wings and white outer tail-feathers

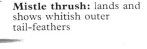

Mistle thrush: lands and shows whitish outer tail-feathers

Skylark: (above) alert on post, crest raised, (below) low profile while feeding

Mistle thrush: bold, often upright stance: often on playing-fields, in parks, etc

Tree pipit's song flight: ascends and 'parachutes' back to same or new perch

Male whitethroat: often secretive, but also appears and sings from exposed perch

Male whitethroat: brief, dancing song-flight from hedgerow or bush

Linnets: often perch on wires; note red (very variable in amount) on breast of male (left)

Linnets: in flight, note small size and white in wings and tail; open ground, roadsides, etc

Tree pipits: rear and side views, very like meadow pipit but best distinguished by song, habitat and constant perching on trees, bushes, etc

Yellowhammer: note long tail in flight

Woodwarbler: usually sings high in trees, 'vibrates' while doing so

Male blackcap: often hard to spot singing in foliage, high or low

Male yellowhammer: sings from exposed perch, often telegraph wires

Wood warbler: song-flights between branches, note long wings and yellow breast

Willow warbler (left) and **chiffchaff** (above): feed and sing in trees, bushes, best distinguished by song

Female blackcap: note brown cap

Willow warbler: 'hooeet' display near nest, keep away!

Blackcap: flies between trees, head pattern usually not seen

Goldcrest: from below, tiny, short-tailed, crest often not visible

Willow warbler or **chiffchaff:** often collects nest material on lawns, etc; note small size and distinctive shape

Tree sparrow: black bib and cheek-spots, white cheeks

Male goldcrest: orange crown only seen well in display, otherwise looks yellow

Bullfinches: male (above), female (below); feeds on buds, often at very tips of branches

Spotted flycatcher: uses all kinds of exposed perches, flies out after insects; note typical upright posture (right)

Spotted flycatcher: hovers to catch insect

Male yellowhammer: rear view, note yellow head, russet rump, white outer tail-feathers

Bullfinches: rear view, male (above), female (left), note white rump, black wings and tail

Wren: very small, active, short cocked tail

Yellowhammers: feed on ground, low posture, often flick tails

Tree sparrows: 'dapper' appearance, brown crown and nape, black cheek-spot, note white collar

Nuthatch: near mud-adorned nest-hole

Nuthatch: dumpy, big-headed, short-tailed; very agile on trees, can climb downwards

Great tits: male singing (left), less black on underside of female (right)

Treecreeper: flies from top of one tree to base of next, note wing-bar in flight

Goldfinches: note wing-pattern (left), red face and breast patches from front (above)

Goldfinch: rear view, yellow wing-bars very conspicuous

Treecreeper: climbs jerkily, often spiralling as ascends trunk

Long-tailed tits: distrinctive shape (below); parties fly in line across gaps in hedges, woods, etc.

Willow tit: broad white cheeks obvious from behind

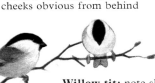

Willow tit: note shape of head and cheek-patches, and pale wing-patch

Coal tits: note head pattern, especially white 'hole' on nape

Marsh tits: with practice, distinguished from willow tit by shape of head and white on cheeks, but voice is usually best distinction between the two

Blue tit: display flights from perch to perch, note wing shape

Male pied wagtails: show aggression, note black back and long tail (below)

Blue tit: note face pattern and yellow underparts

Blue tits: males display during battle on ground

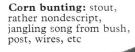

Male pied wagtail: aggressive posture, female has grey back; walks, runs, bobs head and wags tail

Corn bunting: stout, rather nondescript, jangling song from bush, post, wires, etc

Corn bunting: legs dangle as bird flies from song-post

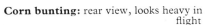

Corn bunting: rear view, looks heavy in flight

Mountain and moorland in spring and summer

These species breed in uplands. Birds of prey are almost always first spotted in flight, when the important features to look for are shape, proportion of wings, body and tail and the way in which they fly. Eagles and buzzards, kestrels and merlin, ravens and crows are species likely to be confused.

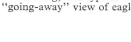

Immature golden eagle and **buzzard** soaring: note size difference.

Immature golden eagle: all dark, varying amount of white in wings and at base of tail.

Eagle

Eagle

Buzzard

Golden eagle and **buzzard** soaring, and typical "going-away" view of eagle.

Golden eagles flapping hard and diving.

Immature golden eagle gliding: wings slightly back, tail half-open.

Golden eagle

Buzzard

Raven

Adult golden eagle: all dark, note prominent head, ample tail and bulging rear edge on wing.
Buzzard: more compact, varying pattern on belly and underwing.
Raven: black, narrow-winged, distinctive tail-shape, buzzard-sized.

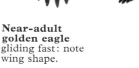

Near-adult golden eagle gliding fast: note wing shape.

Red kite gliding: tail twists and flexes.

Red kite: note colour, conspicuous pale wing-panels; longer-winged than buzzard, distinctive tail.

Adult golden eagle hunting.

Carrion crow (left) and distinctive **hooded crow** (right): compare shape with raven.

Ravens on wing: powerful, active fliers, acrobatic; diagnostic call "pruuk".

Golden eagles overhead, fast sailing or gliding: all dark, note prominence of head and length of tail.

Ravens on ground: large, heavy, massive bill.

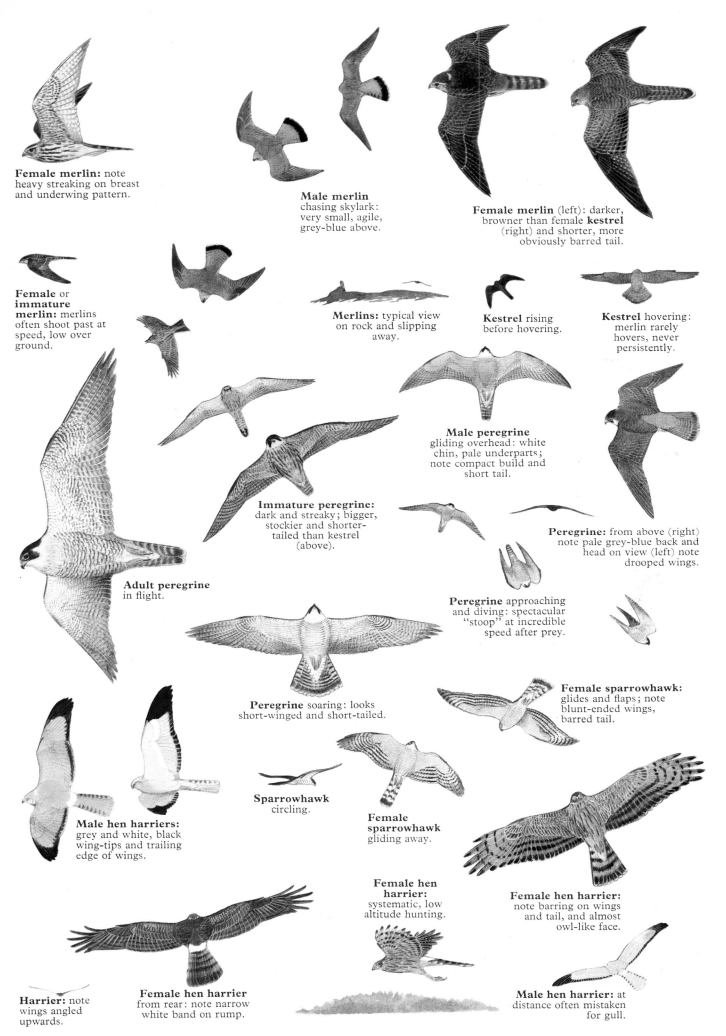

Female merlin: note heavy streaking on breast and underwing pattern.

Male merlin chasing skylark: very small, agile, grey-blue above.

Female merlin (left): darker, browner than female **kestrel** (right) and shorter, more obviously barred tail.

Female or **immature merlin:** merlins often shoot past at speed, low over ground.

Merlins: typical view on rock and slipping away.

Kestrel rising before hovering.

Kestrel hovering: merlin rarely hovers, never persistently.

Male peregrine gliding overhead: white chin, pale underparts; note compact build and short tail.

Immature peregrine: dark and streaky; bigger, stockier and shorter-tailed than kestrel (above).

Peregrine: from above (right) note pale grey-blue back and head on view (left) note drooped wings.

Adult peregrine in flight.

Peregrine approaching and diving: spectacular "stoop" at incredible speed after prey.

Peregrine soaring: looks short-winged and short-tailed.

Female sparrowhawk: glides and flaps; note blunt-ended wings, barred tail.

Male hen harriers: grey and white, black wing-tips and trailing edge of wings.

Sparrowhawk circling.

Female sparrowhawk gliding away.

Female hen harrier: note barring on wings and tail, and almost owl-like face.

Female hen harrier: systematic, low altitude hunting.

Harrier: note wings angled upwards.

Female hen harrier from rear: note narrow white band on rump.

Male hen harrier: at distance often mistaken for gull.

15

Red grouse: plum pudding colour, found on heather moorland.

Red grouse: often seen "gritting" at quiet roadsides.

Ptarmigan: replace grouse on high mountains; tame, well camouflaged grey-and-white.

Ptarmigan: all white in winter, but have distinctive white wings at all seasons.

Cock red grouse

Red grouse approaching: note bowed wings.

Red grouse: flushed and rocketing away, often calling.

Male and female black grouse overhead: both show white underwings.

Black grouse: both sexes perch readily in small trees.

Male black grouse (blackcock) rising: note white underwing, long tail.

Male black grouse from behind: white wing-bars, unique tail shape.

Female black grouse (greyhen): larger, greyer than red grouse, forked tail.

Female black grouse (greyhen): larger, greyer, larger-tailed than red grouse

Curlew: distinctive bill, large size, very vocal.

Curlew from rear: note white rump, pale tail.

Curlew: typical view behind ridge.

Curlew: plumage camouflages bird on grass and moorland.

Golden plover going away: dark, slight wing-bar, very rapid flight.

Greenshank: note white rump in "v" up back, long bill, legs trail beyond tail.

Hooded crows: mainly found in west and north-west Scotland and Ireland; hybridises with carrion crow in central and eastern Highlands.

Short-eared owls: day-hunting, long-winged owls of open country. Note pale underwing, dark patch at bend of wing: frequently hover.

Golden plover: black on belly, pale underwing.

Golden plover: vary from well-marked northern form (left) to black-bellied southern form (right), but many intermediates.

Golden plover: round head, short dark bill, dark legs.

Golden plover: gold-spangled upperparts, slight wing-bar.

Dotterel: note blackish crown and white eye-stripe.

Red-throated diver (left): small lochs and pools; **black-throated** usually larger waters.

Dotterel: note white breast-band, chestnut lower breast and dark belly.

Lapwing: often common on marginal uplands.

Dotterel: white eye-stripe and chin, very dark underparts.

Grey wagtail: note grey back, yellow on rump; found on hill streams.

Meadow pipit: note white outer tail-feathers.

Skylark singing

Ring ouzels: note grey in wing-feathers, brownish female has pale crescent on breast; rocky hillsides.

Skylark from rear: white rear edge to wing, white outer tail-feathers.

Meadow pipit: streaky plumage, distinctive "tseep-tseep" calls.

Dunlin landing; distinct black belly in summer.

Wheatear: only small bird in these habitats with flashing white rump.

Twite: like dark female linnet but streakier, buff throat, yellowish bill.

Female stonechat (above) and **female whinchat** (below): note latter's wing and tail markings.

Dunlin in breeding plumage: chestnut above, note white wing-bars.

Twite: male (right) compared with female (left) male's pinkish rump hard to see in field; distinctive nasal "twite" calls.

Common sandpipers: wings stiffly bowed in flight, conspicuous white wing-bars; streams and lake-sides.

Female linnet: shows much more white in flight than twite.

Dipper found on or along rocky streams.

Coasts and cliffs in spring and summer

Waders in breeding plumage are boldly marked and quite easy to distinguish once their patterns have been learned. Terns require practice and patience. Although relatively easy at their breeding colonies, auks (puffin, razorbill and guillemots) are often difficult to identify when they are flying offshore.

Oystercatchers: large, pied, noisy birds.

Avocet: mostly white; unmistakable.

Ringed plover: "butterfly" display flight.

Ringed plover: sandy-brown above, white wing-bar.

Dunlin: streaked chestnut back, white wing-bars, longish bill.

Redshank: only medium-sized wader with white rump and hindwing; noisy.

Sanderling: brighter wing-bar than dunlin, less chestnut, short bill.

Redshank: speckled brown, pale belly, obvious bright red legs.

Turnstone: unique black, white and chestnut pattern on wings and back.

Knot: medium-sized, mottled chestnut on back, faint white wing-bar.

Ringed plover: note head pattern and black breast-band; yellow legs.

Summer turnstone: unmistakable tortoise-shell pattern; note transitional plumage of sub-adult (right).

Knot: stocky, short-legged, pinkish to russet underparts.

Dunlin: chestnut back, black belly — much variation.

Sanderling: white belly, short, straight black bill.

Shelduck: unmistakable; looks pied, near goose-size.

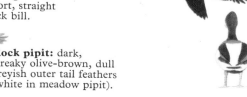

Rock pipit: dark, streaky olive-brown, dull greyish outer tail feathers (white in meadow pipit).

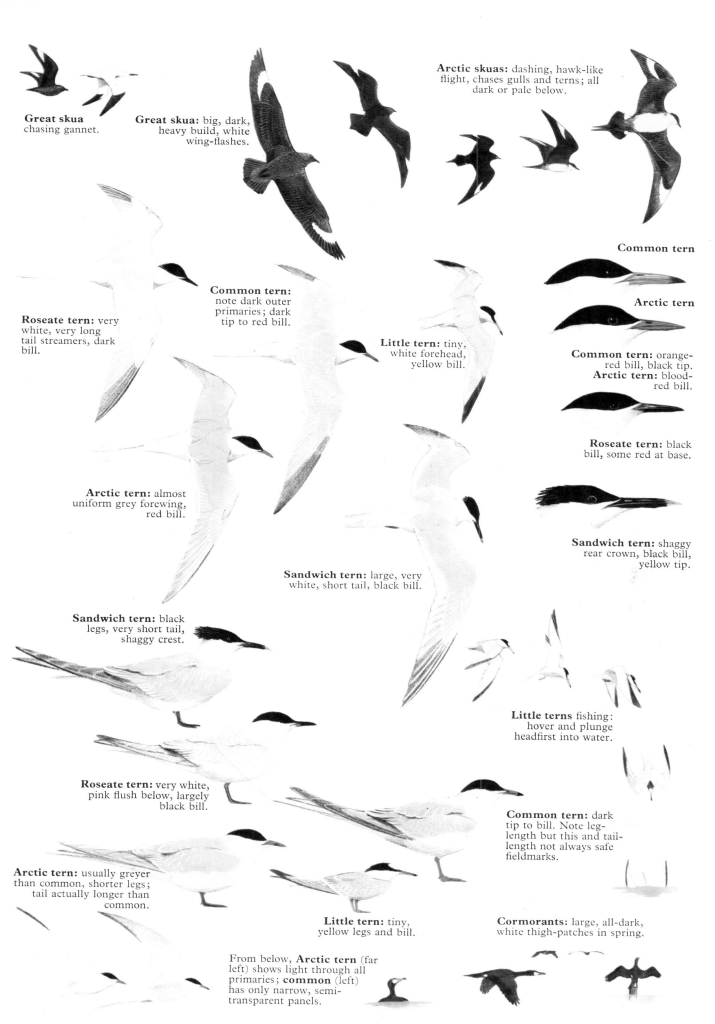

Great skua chasing gannet.

Great skua: big, dark, heavy build, white wing-flashes.

Arctic skuas: dashing, hawk-like flight, chases gulls and terns; all dark or pale below.

Common tern

Arctic tern

Common tern: note dark outer primaries; dark tip to red bill.

Common tern: orange-red bill, black tip.
Arctic tern: blood-red bill.

Roseate tern: very white, very long tail streamers, dark bill.

Little tern: tiny, white forehead, yellow bill.

Roseate tern: black bill, some red at base.

Arctic tern: almost uniform grey forewing, red bill.

Sandwich tern: shaggy rear crown, black bill, yellow tip.

Sandwich tern: large, very white, short tail, black bill.

Sandwich tern: black legs, very short tail, shaggy crest.

Little terns fishing: hover and plunge headfirst into water.

Roseate tern: very white, pink flush below, largely black bill.

Common tern: dark tip to bill. Note leg-length but this and tail-length not always safe fieldmarks.

Arctic tern: usually greyer than common, shorter legs; tail actually longer than common.

Little tern: tiny, yellow legs and bill.

Cormorants: large, all-dark, white thigh-patches in spring.

From below, **Arctic tern** (far left) shows light through all primaries; **common** (left) has only narrow, semi-transparent panels.

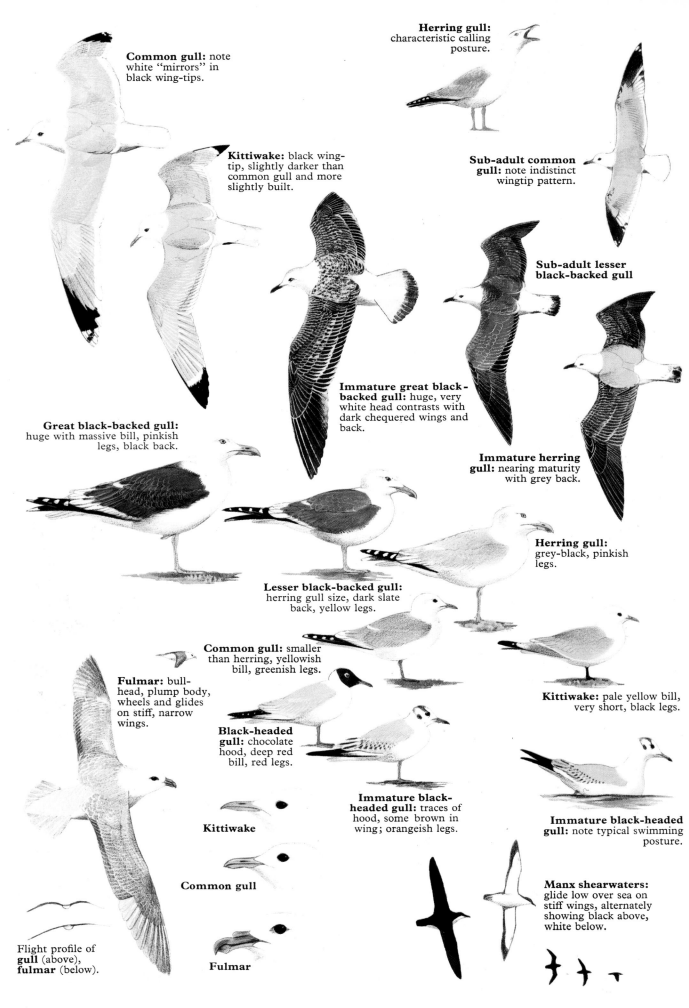

Common gull: note white "mirrors" in black wing-tips.

Herring gull: characteristic calling posture.

Kittiwake: black wing-tip, slightly darker than common gull and more slightly built.

Sub-adult common gull: note indistinct wingtip pattern.

Sub-adult lesser black-backed gull

Immature great black-backed gull: huge, very white head contrasts with dark chequered wings and back.

Great black-backed gull: huge with massive bill, pinkish legs, black back.

Immature herring gull: nearing maturity with grey back.

Herring gull: grey-black, pinkish legs.

Lesser black-backed gull: herring gull size, dark slate back, yellow legs.

Common gull: smaller than herring, yellowish bill, greenish legs.

Kittiwake: pale yellow bill, very short, black legs.

Fulmar: bull-head, plump body, wheels and glides on stiff, narrow wings.

Black-headed gull: chocolate hood, deep red bill, red legs.

Immature black-headed gull: traces of hood, some brown in wing; orangeish legs.

Immature black-headed gull: note typical swimming posture.

Kittiwake

Common gull

Manx shearwaters: glide low over sea on stiff wings, alternately showing black above, white below.

Flight profile of **gull** (above), **fulmar** (below).

Fulmar

Puffin: greyish cheeks, stands upright on orange legs.

Shape of head and bill best feature for separating **razorbill** (left) and **guillemot** (right) when flying.

Puffin: smaller and longer-winged than other auks, head pattern usually obvious.

Guillemot (left) and **razorbill** (right) leaving cliff: note large, obvious feet.

Razorbill: black and white, distinctive bill shape.

Guillemot: much browner than razorbill; note bill shape.

Distant adult **gannet:** conspicuously white above, black wing-ends.

Flight profiles of **chough** (top) and **jackdaw** (above).

Adult gannet: unmistakable, very large, angular white bird.

Ravens: long, rather narrow wings, wedge-shaped tail, massive bill; much larger than crow.

Chough (right): broader wings than **jackdaw** (left), widespread "fingers", no grey on head.

Chough (far left) is blacker than **jackdaw** (left) with red bill and legs.

Shags in summer: dark bottle-green (black at distance), short crest in spring.

Shag (left) slimmer than **cormorant** (right), slighter bill, no white on face.

Rock dove: note white rump panel, dark bars on inner wing; feral pigeon often almost identical. Found extreme north and west of Britain and Ireland.

Eiders: male unmistakable; Female large, dark brown seaduck, angular head and bill, dives.

Black guillemot: all black, small, with white wing-patches, orange legs. Found close inshore.

Razorbill (left): note head-shape, tail often cocked when swimming, **Guillemot** (right): looks longer, with larger, finer bill; lower in water.

Puffin: dumpy, greyish cheeks, unique bill.

Shores and estuaries in autumn and winter

Waders, particularly the smaller species, are a very difficult group to learn. Wing- and tail-patterns are the key identification features. Get to know the very common dunlin well and other small waders will be learned more easily. Swimming birds can be identified by their plumage patterns and how they sit in the water. Immature gulls are another difficult group identified by wing- and tail-patterns.

Summer   Winter

Sanderling: small, very white, fast-running. Found on sandy shores.

Purple sandpiper: dumpy, short legs, very tame. Found on rocks, breakwaters, etc.

Little stint: tiny, "tittit" call. Immature (below) has whitish back markings, adult very like small dunlin.

Dunlin: commonest small wader. Note variation — winter adults much paler than immatures. Sanderling (bottom) always much whiter in winter.

Curlew sandpiper: similar to dunlin but larger with white rump. Characteristic "chirrip" call.

Turnstone: stocky, dark breast and back, chestnut above in summer. Found on open and rocky shores.

Knot: medium-sized wader, very grey, indistinct wing-bar, greyish rump. See also grey plover.

Dunlin (far left) and immature **little stint:** compare size, back-markings, bills.

Little stints: clean white below, very short bills. Immature (left), winter adult (above).

Ringed plover: combination of back-colour, wing and tail markings distinguish from other small waders.

Turnstone: pied back and wing patterns, twittering call.

Dunlin: variable in plumage, and bill shape and size.

Purple sandpiper: darkest wader, indistinct white markings.

Curlew sandpiper: more slender and slightly larger than dunlin, longer decurved bill.

Knot: larger than other waders on this page, mainly grey in winter, straight bill, rather short legs.

Common sandpiper: note markings, but best told by distinctive flight — flicking on stiffly bowed wings, low over water.

Black-tailed godwit (A): white rump patch and wing-bar. Feet project well beyond tail.

Bar-tailed godwit (B): white 'V' on back similar to whimbrel.

Godwits: black-tailed (A) has much longer bill and legs.

Black-tailed godwit (A), **bar-tailed godwit** (B): note pied patterning of A and unmarked wings of B.

Godwits and **oystercatcher** from rear: black-tailed (A) similar to oystercatcher but lacks "V" on back.

Grey plovers (above and right): white rump, round head and short bill. Note black armpits.

Grey plover: large, stocky grey wader with dark bill and eye, black legs.

Ruffs: female **reeve**, male **ruff**, note upright stance, rather short bill. Plumage very variable. White oval on sides of tail (left), no wing-bar.

Greenshank (C): very often has white head and neck, slightly upturned bill.
Spotted redshank (D): paler than redshank (E), longer legs and bill, more slender proportions.

Greenshank (D), **spotted redshank** (C) and **redshank** (E): note back-patternings at long range.

Greenshank (D): note extent of white rump and compare with **spotted redshank** (C); tail of greenshank looks almost white, darker on spotted redshank.
Redshank (E): always has prominent white wing-bars.

Curlew: very large, white rump, long decurved bill (but variable in length).
Whimbrel: smaller, shorter bill, faster wing-beats, striped crown but this is often very hard to see.

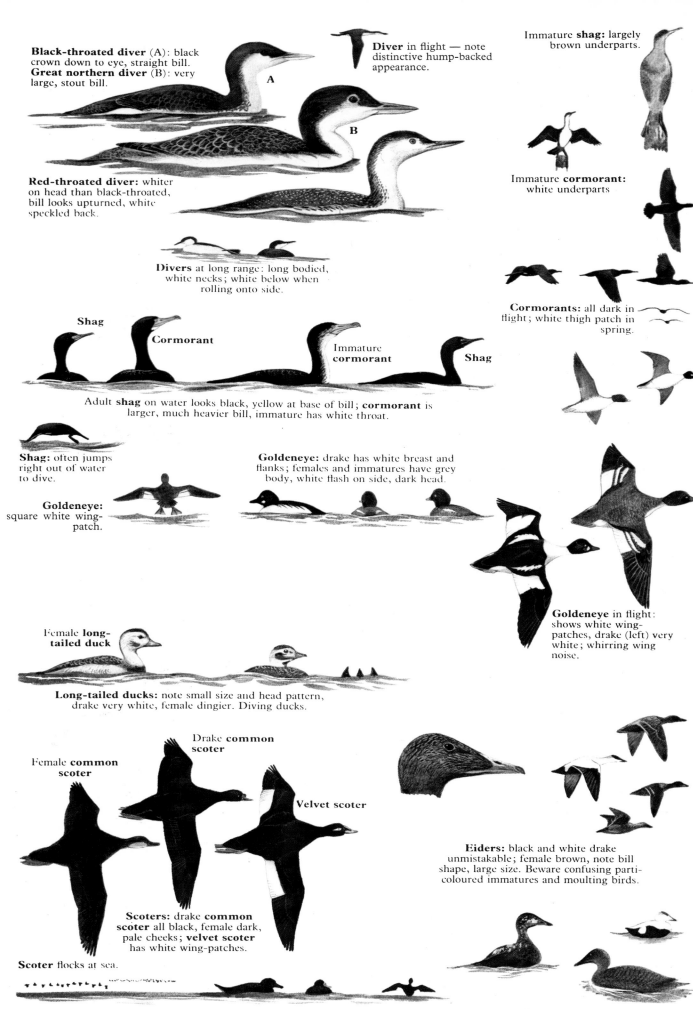

Black-throated diver (A): black crown down to eye, straight bill.
Great northern diver (B): very large, stout bill.

Diver in flight — note distinctive hump-backed appearance.

Immature **shag**: largely brown underparts.

Red-throated diver: whiter on head than black-throated, bill looks upturned, white speckled back.

Immature **cormorant**: white underparts

Divers at long range: long bodied, white necks; white below when rolling onto side.

Cormorants: all dark in flight; white thigh patch in spring.

Shag

Cormorant

Immature cormorant

Shag

Adult **shag** on water looks black, yellow at base of bill; **cormorant** is larger, much heavier bill, immature has white throat.

Shag: often jumps right out of water to dive.

Goldeneye: drake has white breast and flanks; females and immatures have grey body, white flash on side, dark head.

Goldeneye: square white wing-patch.

Goldeneye in flight: shows white wing-patches, drake (left) very white; whirring wing noise.

Female **long-tailed duck**

Long-tailed ducks: note small size and head pattern, drake very white, female dingier. Diving ducks.

Drake **common scoter**

Female **common scoter**

Velvet scoter

Eiders: black and white drake unmistakable; female brown, note bill shape, large size. Beware confusing parti-coloured immatures and moulting birds.

Scoters: drake **common scoter** all black, female dark, pale cheeks; **velvet scoter** has white wing-patches.

Scoter flocks at sea.

24

Oystercatchers flying: unmistakable large, pied waders.

Immature **shelduck**: large, whitish, lacks full markings of adult (behind).

Lapwings: pied wader, but note very characteristic wing-shape.

Lapwing: note crest and white sides of head.

Oystercatchers at rest: white chin-mark in winter.

Red-necked grebe: similar to small great crested, but yellowish bill, black crown down to eye, neck often greyish contrasting with white cheeks.

Black-necked and **Slavonian grebes**: postures common to both, dive frequently.

Slavonian grebe (top), **black-necked** (above): note bill shape and extent of black on crown.

Twite: small, mainly brown, linnet-like finch, yellow bill, some white on wings. Forms flocks.

Brent geese: small bill, black head and neck, dark upper-parts, grey belly. Swimming bird is dark-bellied race.

Male **snow bunting**

Brent geese from rear: look all dark, white chevron on tail.

Female **snow bunting**

Skylark

Shore lark

Snow buntings (above and below): males whitest, females dingier, but always have much white on wings.
Juvenile (left): much browner, note white on outer tail feathers.

Twite flying up from shore: note unmarked tail, pinkish rump sometimes obvious.

Shore lark: compare pattern of wings and tail with larger browner skylark (above).

Twite (left) and **shore larks** (right and below): note latter's pale underparts and face-markings.

Snow buntings (below): creep low over shore, often feed with twite.

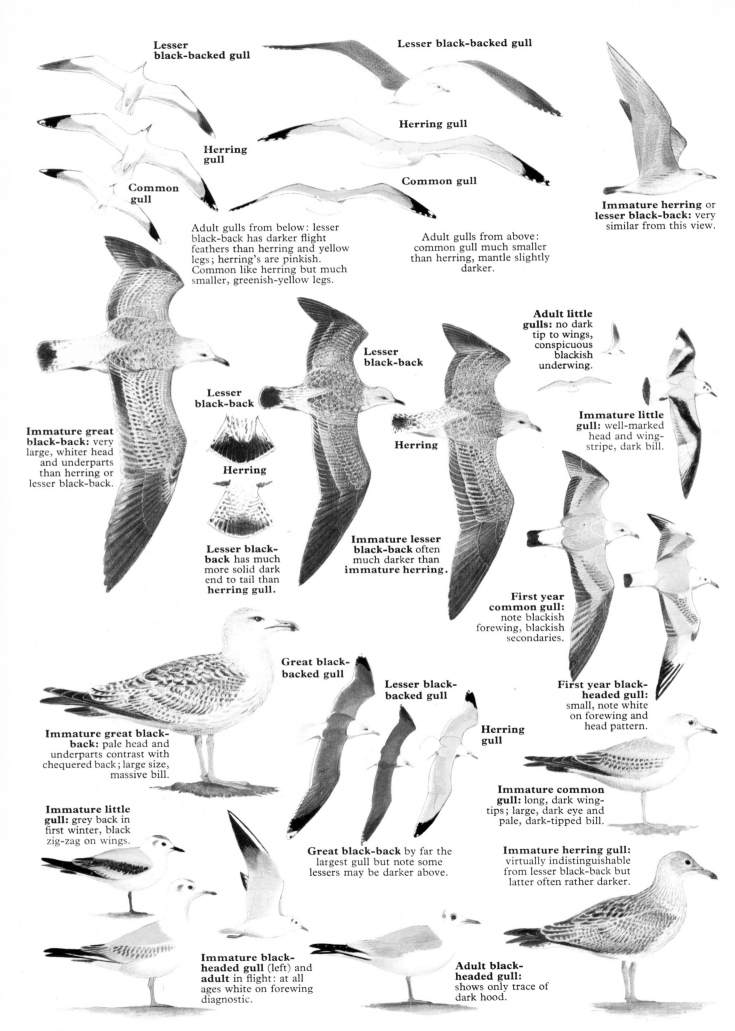

Lesser black-backed gull

Lesser black-backed gull

Herring gull

Herring gull

Common gull

Common gull

Immature herring or **lesser black-back:** very similar from this view.

Adult gulls from below: lesser black-back has darker flight feathers than herring and yellow legs; herring's are pinkish. Common like herring but much smaller, greenish-yellow legs.

Adult gulls from above: common gull much smaller than herring, mantle slightly darker.

Adult little gulls: no dark tip to wings, conspicuous blackish underwing.

Lesser black-back

Lesser black-back

Lesser black-back

Herring

Immature great black-back: very large, whiter head and underparts than herring or lesser black-back.

Lesser black-back has much more solid dark end to tail than herring gull.

Immature lesser black-back often much darker than **immature herring.**

Immature little gull: well-marked head and wing-stripe, dark bill.

First year common gull: note blackish forewing, blackish secondaries.

Great black-backed gull

Lesser black-backed gull

Herring gull

First year black-headed gull: small, note white on forewing and head pattern.

Immature great black-back: pale head and underparts contrast with chequered back; large size, massive bill.

Immature little gull: grey back in first winter, black zig-zag on wings.

Great black-back by far the largest gull but note some lessers may be darker above.

Immature common gull: long, dark wing-tips; large, dark eye and pale, dark-tipped bill.

Immature herring gull: virtually indistinguishable from lesser black-back but latter often rather darker.

Immature black-headed gull (left) and **adult** in flight: at all ages white on forewing diagnostic.

Adult black-headed gull: shows only trace of dark hood.

Inland waters in winter

Colour and shape are the main pointers to birds on the water. Note the way in which species differ in their swimming positions. In flight, look at the patterns of wings and the amount of colour on the undersides.

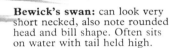

Whooper swan

Bewick's swan

Whooper is larger and longer-necked than **Bewick's** but latter appears equally tall when alert and neck is fully extended.

Bill shape and colouring is important in swan identification: see drawings below.

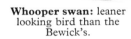

Juvenile mute swan: all mutes have characteristic curve to neck, those of other swans being far straighter.

Whooper swan

Bewick's swan

Juvenile whooper

Juvenile Bewick's

Juvenile mute

Whooper swan: leaner looking bird than the Bewick's.

Bewick's swan: can look very short necked, also note rounded head and bill shape. Often sits on water with tail held high.

Moorhens on land: white flank-stripe and under-tail are characteristic.

Moorhens on water: jerky head action, often flick tail to show white "horseshoe" below.

Coot on land: all black with outsized feet.

Coots swimming: all black with white bill and frontal shield; characteristic rounded shape.

Coot: rather laboured flight, large feet hanging or trailing.

Coot on water.

Bearded tit: small, mainly tawny bird with long tail and whirring flight; "pinging" call.

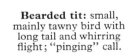

Bearded tits: often active at reed-tops.

Carrion crow: black, no white on face, heavy bill. Sometimes gregarious in winter.

Kingfisher: unmistakable, fishes from perch or may hover over water.

Female reed bunting: note white outer tail-feathers, chestnut on "shoulders" and streaked back-pattern; jerky flight.

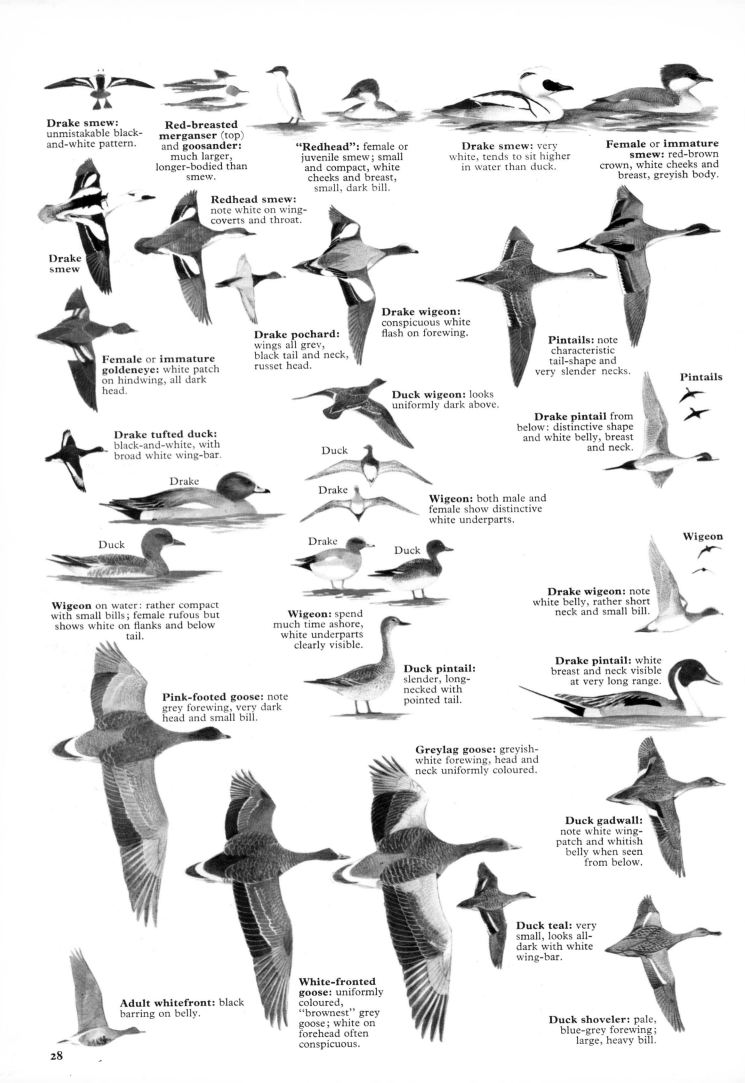

Drake smew: unmistakable black-and-white pattern.

Red-breasted merganser (top) and **goosander:** much larger, longer-bodied than smew.

"Redhead": female or juvenile smew; small and compact, white cheeks and breast, small, dark bill.

Drake smew: very white, tends to sit higher in water than duck.

Female or **immature smew:** red-brown crown, white cheeks and breast, greyish body.

Redhead smew: note white on wing-coverts and throat.

Drake smew

Female or **immature goldeneye:** white patch on hindwing, all dark head.

Drake pochard: wings all grey, black tail and neck, russet head.

Drake wigeon: conspicuous white flash on forewing.

Pintails: note characteristic tail-shape and very slender necks.

Pintails

Drake pintail from below: distinctive shape and white belly, breast and neck.

Duck wigeon: looks uniformly dark above.

Drake tufted duck: black-and-white, with broad white wing-bar.

Drake

Duck

Duck

Drake

Wigeon: both male and female show distinctive white underparts.

Wigeon

Drake

Duck

Wigeon on water: rather compact with small bills; female rufous but shows white on flanks and below tail.

Wigeon: spend much time ashore, white underparts clearly visible.

Drake wigeon: note white belly, rather short neck and small bill.

Duck pintail: slender, long-necked with pointed tail.

Drake pintail: white breast and neck visible at very long range.

Pink-footed goose: note grey forewing, very dark head and small bill.

Greylag goose: greyish-white forewing, head and neck uniformly coloured.

Duck gadwall: note white wing-patch and whitish belly when seen from below.

Duck teal: very small, looks all-dark with white wing-bar.

Adult whitefront: black barring on belly.

White-fronted goose: uniformly coloured, "brownest" grey goose; white on forehead often conspicuous.

Duck shoveler: pale, blue-grey forewing; large, heavy bill.

Cormorants: large, all dark (but immature has whitish throat), heavy, tilted-up bills.

Red-throated diver: white throat and neck in winter; characteristic "up-tilted" shape to bill.

Shags: more slender necked and finer billed than cormorant. Often jump clear of water before diving, unlike divers.

Great crested grebes: note low and high profile.

Great crested grebe in flight: characteristic wing-pattern and trailing feet.

Great crested grebe: pink bill, black crown does not extend down to eye.

Herons in flight: large broad wings and deep, slow wing-beats; neck retracted, feet trail beyond tail.

Herons: perched head hunched into shoulders, upright stance.

Black-necked grebe

Slavonian grebe

Slavonian grebe shows less white on wing than **black-necked,** and sometimes small white "shoulder patches"

Little grebe: tiny, dumpy build, pale on neck and flanks.

Slavonian grebe: small size, very white cheeks and neck.

Black-necked grebe: less well-defined cap, dingier cheeks and sides of neck.

Dipper: white bib, stocky build, white eyelid often conspicuous.

Dippers: open wings while feeding on water; rapid, low flight on small, dark, short wings.

Meadow pipit: white outer-tail feathers in flight; often circles up calling "tseep-tseep" when flushed.

Meadow pipit: streaked brown back, white outer tail feathers.

Snipe: "towers" when flushed, zig-zags up and away; harsh calls.

Jack snipe: flushes at close range, soon drops down again; silent.

Jack snipe

Jack snipe: smaller, darker, shorter billed than snipe, with well-patterned back; lacks white on edge of wing and tail.

Snipe

Water rail when flushed: looks all dark, weak flight, trailing legs.

Juvenile pied wagtail: shows only traces of adult's head pattern.

Snipe from below: Jack snipe has plain underwing, much shorter bill, shorter legs.

Water rail "end-on": remarkably slender, note buffish-white undertail.

Water rail: in poor view long bill and rather dark appearance diagnostic; barring on flank often visible.

Jack snipe on ground: very small and dumpy, with peculiar bouncing feeding action.

Inland waters in spring and summer

Lakes, gravel-pits, rivers, streams and marshes are all good places to see birds. Waterside vegetation in summer is the breeding place of several small perching birds, which can be sorted out by voice and behaviour as well as appearance.

Sedge warbler: typically sings from perch, often hidden in vegetation. But in song-flight (above left) rises and "parachutes" down.

Sedge warbler: creamy strip over eye, streaked back and tawny rump. Breeds in vegetation bordering water

Reed warblers: uniformly coloured above, paler below. Breed in reeds, osiers and waterside vegetation.

Grasshopper warbler: more often heard than seen, long reeling song on one note.

Grasshopper warbler: note rounded tail and streaked back.

Cock reed bunting: black and white head pattern.

Bearded tits: small, very long-tailed tawny birds of reedbeds, male (far right) with grey head and strikingly patterned back; "pinging" calls.

Hen reed bunting: pattern of cheeks and moustachial stripe.

Reed bunting: in flight rather jerky, note obvious outer tail-feathers.

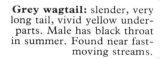

Grey wagtail: slender, very long tail, vivid yellow under-parts. Male has black throat in summer. Found near fast-moving streams.

Yellow wagtails: note white outer tail feathers even visible in flight (below left).

Grey wagtails: undulating flight, note yellow rump and under tail.

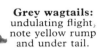

Little ringed plover (far left): smaller than **ringed plover** (left), more white on forehead and narrower breast band.

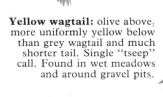

Yellow wagtail: olive above, more uniformly yellow below than grey wagtail and much shorter tail. Single "tseep" call. Found in wet meadows and around gravel pits.

Ringed plover: more black on forehead, yellow on bill and orange-yellow legs. Occasionally breeds on gravel pits but more a coastal bird.

Little ringed plover: white between crown, yellow eye-ring, almost all-dark bill and legs flesh or greenish-yellow. Often breeds inland on shingle edges of gravel pits and reservoirs.

Little ringed plover: (left): lacks wing bar.

Heron: large, long-legged and long-necked with dagger-shaped bill. Although usually seen beside water, does perch in trees.

Herons: in flight; note large round-ended wings, retracted neck, feet projected beyond tail; slow, heavy wing-beats.

Heronry: **herons** are colonial breeders, building large nests in treetops.

Greylag goose: note heavy bill and uniform colour of head, neck and underparts. Birds seen in summer in England are feral.

Canada goose: grey-brown with black neck and head and distinctive markings. Found on lakes, gravel pits and broad rivers, grazes on farmland.

Canada goose: (rear view) landing, note tail pattern and uniformly dark wings.

Greylag: in flight, note off-white forewings.

Snipe: gives short rasping call when flushed and rapidly zigzags away, often climbing high. Found marshes and wet meadows.

Dipper: rear view, fast direct flight, dumpy on short wings.

Dipper: feeds in or under swift-flowing water, even where it is quite deep.

Snipe: "drumming" display-flight has climax in near-vertical dives with a rapid beating produced by vibrating outer tail-feathers.

Mute swan with cygnets: latter are ash-grey or, very rarely, white.

Kingfisher: note brilliant colours, short tail, large head and bill. May hover like big hummingbird before diving, but more often fishes from perch above water.

Mute swan: note raised wings, curved neck and knob at base of orange (or pinkish) bill. Basal knob on female is smaller.

Great crested grebe: striped young often ride on parent's back.

Little grebe or **dabchick:** tiny round-bodied, looks all-dark at distance or in poor light. Dives when disturbed. Found lakes, rivers and gravel pits.

Great crested grebe: dives from surface for fish. Note head-plumage and slender white neck. Found broad rivers, lakes and gravel pits.

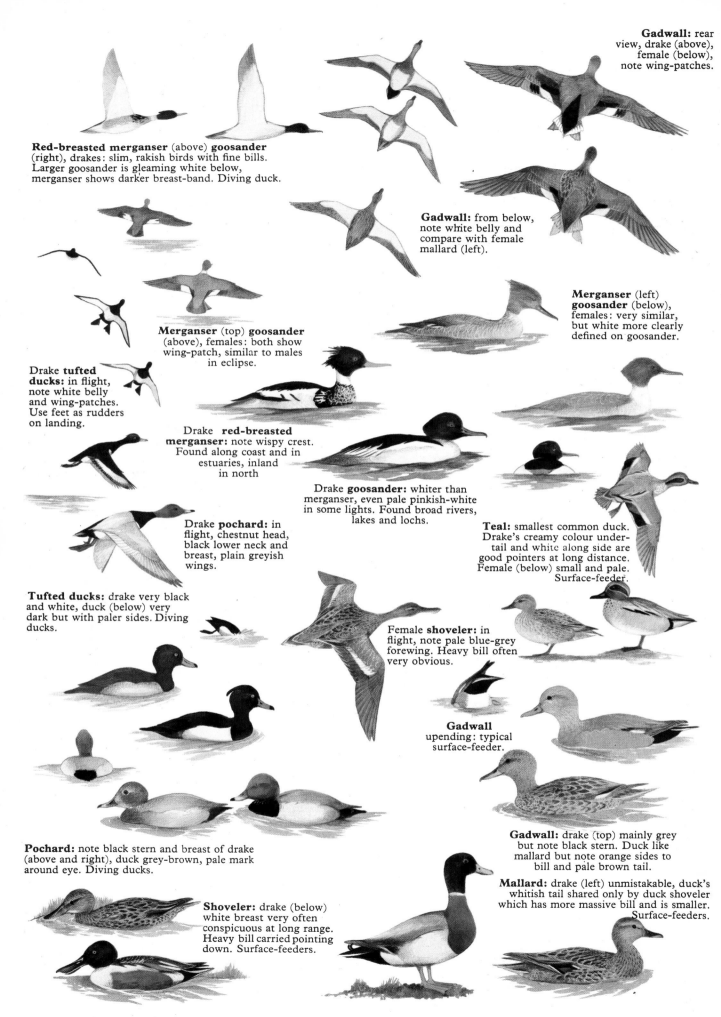

Gadwall: rear view, drake (above), female (below), note wing-patches.

Red-breasted merganser (above) **goosander** (right), drakes: slim, rakish birds with fine bills. Larger goosander is gleaming white below, merganser shows darker breast-band. Diving duck.

Gadwall: from below, note white belly and compare with female mallard (left).

Merganser (left) **goosander** (below), females: very similar, but white more clearly defined on goosander.

Merganser (top) **goosander** (above), females: both show wing-patch, similar to males in eclipse.

Drake **tufted ducks:** in flight, note white belly and wing-patches. Use feet as rudders on landing.

Drake **red-breasted merganser:** note wispy crest. Found along coast and in estuaries, inland in north

Drake **pochard:** in flight, chestnut head, black lower neck and breast, plain greyish wings.

Drake **goosander:** whiter than merganser, even pale pinkish-white in some lights. Found broad rivers, lakes and lochs.

Teal: smallest common duck. Drake's creamy colour under-tail and white along side are good pointers at long distance. Female (below) small and pale. Surface-feeder.

Tufted ducks: drake very black and white, duck (below) very dark but with paler sides. Diving ducks.

Female **shoveler:** in flight, note pale blue-grey forewing. Heavy bill often very obvious.

Gadwall upending: typical surface-feeder.

Pochard: note black stern and breast of drake (above and right), duck grey-brown, pale mark around eye. Diving ducks.

Gadwall: drake (top) mainly grey but note black stern. Duck like mallard but note orange sides to bill and pale brown tail.

Mallard: drake (left) unmistakable, duck's whitish tail shared only by duck shoveler which has more massive bill and is smaller. Surface-feeders.

Shoveler: drake (below) white breast very often conspicuous at long range. Heavy bill carried pointing down. Surface-feeders.